THE NUMBER STORY

BOOK THREE

Numbers Introduce Eleven Twelve, and the Teens

written and illustrated by

MISS ANNA

Hello there.
Remember us?
We are the Numbers you can trust.

We are here today to share
more Number stories.

Numbers Eleven to Twenty will tell us a bit,
About why Thirteen is a *PARTY*
and Eighteen is a *HIT*!

Every number is important,
they cheerily say.
'Unforgettable!' writes cheeky Twelve,
'in every way.'

In a book of world history,
they sit on every page.

They decorate cars

and speeches.

They celebrate
the age.

A number adds meaning
to every and all things,

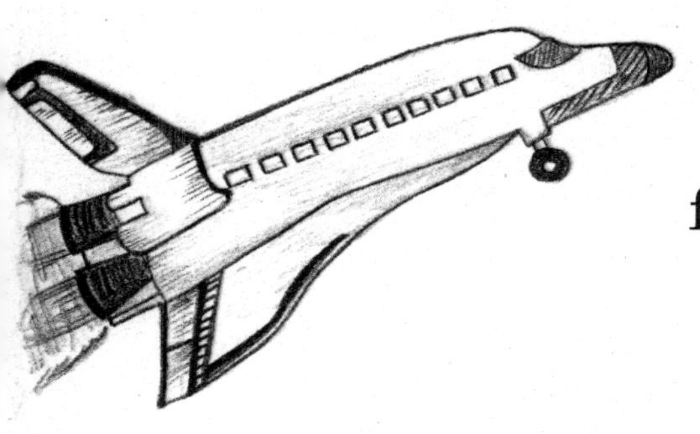

from rocket ships

to chess pawns,

to queens

and to kings.

So, here, in this book,
you'll find tales and stories

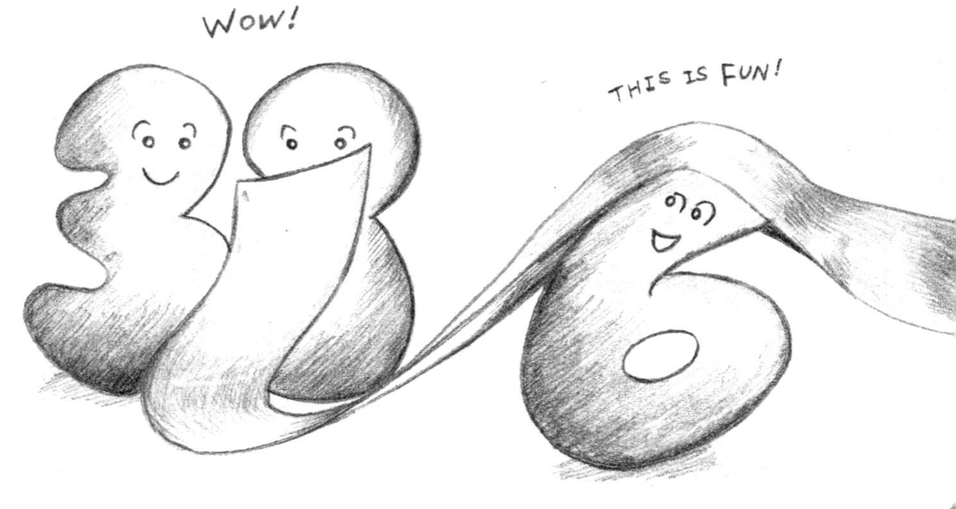

Of numbers Eleven to Twenty
and their favorite memories.

Come read with us!

My number name is

11

Eleven

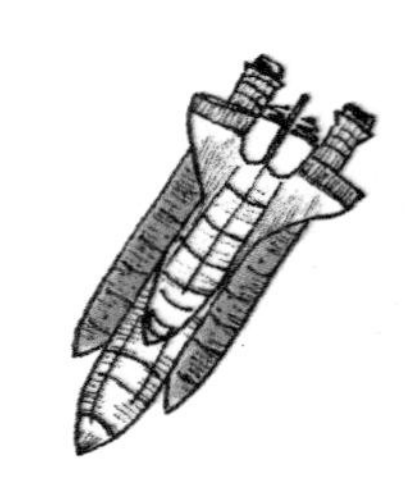

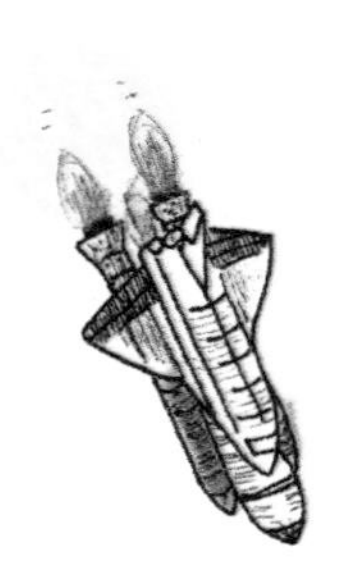
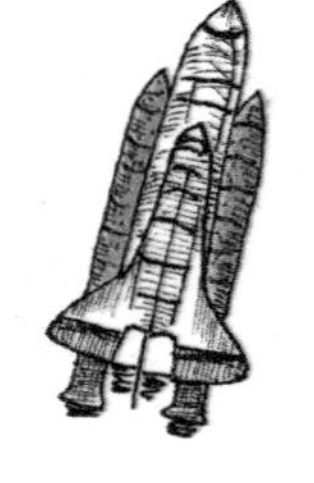

Can you say
e – le – ven?

Apollo 11 was a **rocket** that zoomed to the **moon.**

My number name is

12

Twelve

Can you say twelve?

12 o'clock is time for lunch.

After 12 o'clock, we say,

'Good afternoon.'

My number name is

13

Thirteen

Can you say thir-teen?

At 13, many Jewish boys enjoy

a 'Coming of Age' party

with cakes, toasts, and bright festoons.

festoon: a hanging wreath or garland (of flowers, leaves, etc.) used for decorations and celebrations

My number name is

14

Fourteen

Can you say four-teen?

February 14th is Valentine's Day,
a day full of flowers, 'I Love You' cards,
and heart-shaped balloons.

My number name is

15

Fifteen

Can you say fif-teen?

The 15th is the middle of the month.

The 16th is the next day

and is coming up soon...

My number name is

16

Sixteen

Can you say six-teen?

In the game of chess,

a team of 16 makes their move.

'Protect the King!' they all shout,

'or else our kingdom will lay in ruins.'

My number name is
17
Seventeen
Can you say
se-ven-teen?

Insects called cicadas can stay hidden

in the dirt for up to 17 years!

'When should I pop out?' they wonder.

'The weather is fine from April to June...'

My number name is

18

Eighteen

Can you say eigh-teen?

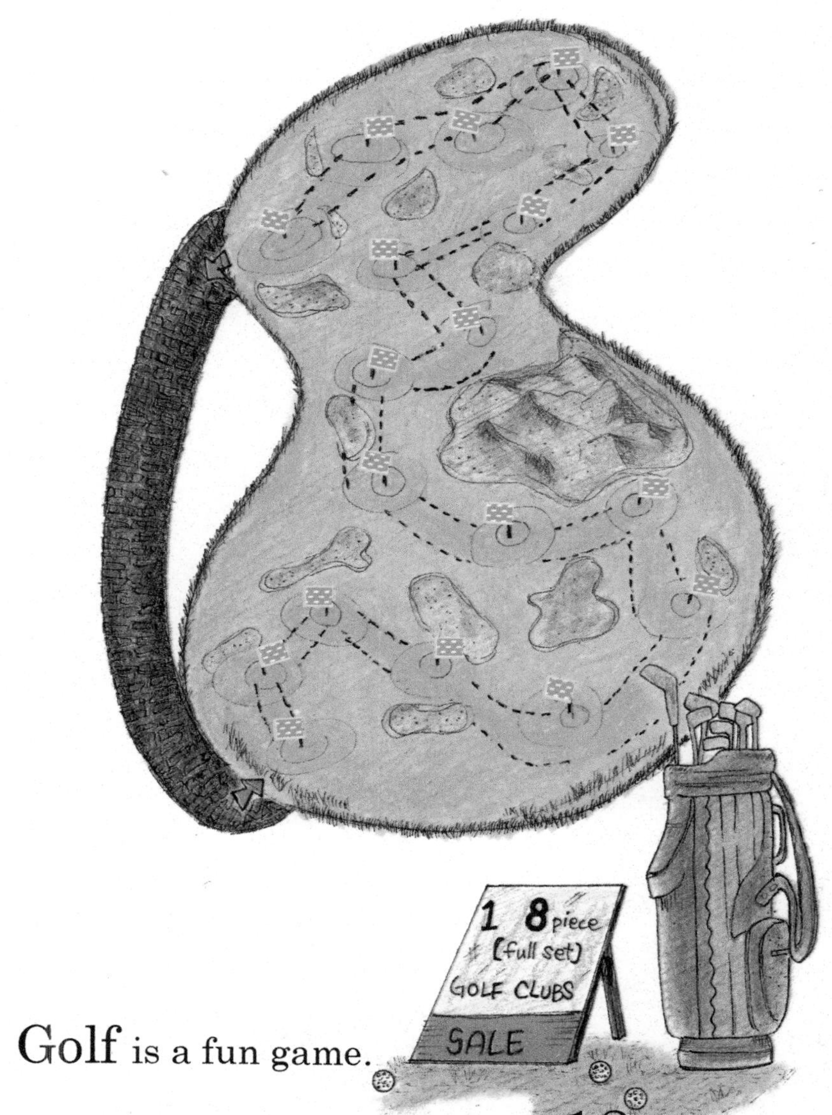

Golf is a fun game.

You must get the ball into 18 holes.

Yes, all 18. And remember to avoid

the traps like bunkers and dunes!

My number name is

19

Nineteen

Can you say nine-teen?

When you turn 19,

it will be your last teen year.

The time has come to follow your

dreams and seek your fortune.

My number name is

20

Twenty

Can you say twen-ty?

The number **20**

can be called a **score**.

Abraham Lincoln, America's 16th president,

told of 'Four score and seven years'.

How many years is that?

Doesn't it carry a poetic tune?

Counting Fun

We Numbers enjoy counting eleven to twenty.

11 Eleven rockets blasting

12 Twelve clocks tick-tocking

13 Thirteen cupcakes for celebrating

14 Fourteen hearts connecting

15 Fifteen sports cars racing

Were you able to find all 14 hearts?
Were you able to count 15 racing cars?

16 Sixteen chess pawns battling

17 Seventeen cicadas sunning

18 Eighteen golf clubs playing

19 Nineteen bright stars shining

20 Twenty drummers drumming

We enjoyed every Number's story,
every party, every trip,
Celebrating with 13,
flying 11's rocket ship.

So, every number is important.
Every number is fun.

Eleven to Twenty comes right after Ten,
and each has two numbers not one.

Thank you

for joining us for this story time.

Truly delightful were

We'll see you in the next book.

There will be choco-chip cookies for free!

But, for now, goodbye,

from the Numbers

in the 0-20 Number Tree.

We are glad they sent us
their memoir.

Aren't you?

Au

Revoir!
Goodbye until we meet again...
(Pronounced au-oo-re-vu-a)

FOR you!
Love,
NUMBERS
tea
We made
sure it is
Caffeine Free.

Copyright © 2017 by Jieeun Woo
Illustrations © Jieeun Woo

Layout by Jieeun Woo | Lumpy Publishing
Edited by Billy Bob Buttons

All rights reserved. No part of this book may be reproduced or transmitted in any form or by any means whatsoever, including photocopying, recording or by any information storage and retrieval system, without written permission from the publisher and/or author: missanna@missannabooks.com.

Library of Congress Control Number: 2017909164

Names: Woo, Jieeun, author, illustrator.
Title: The Number story 3 : numbers introduce eleven , twelve , and the teens; The Number story 4 : numbers teach children their ordinal names / written and illustrated by Miss Anna.
Series: The Number Story
Description: Portland, OR: Lumpy Publishing, 2017.
Identifiers: ISBN 978-1-945977-01-5 | LCCN 2017909164
Summary: The pictures and rhymes present stories which introduce numbers 11-20.
Ordinal numbers are also introduced as Numbers attend friendly games.
Subjects: LCSH Numeration--Juvenile literature. | Number concept--Juvenile literature. |
Counting--Juvenile literature. | BISAC JUVENILE NONFICTION / Concepts / Counting & Numbers
Classification: LCC QA141.3 .M57 2017 | DDC 513--dc23

Publisher: Lumpy Publishing
Website: www.missannabooks.com
Email: missanna@missannabooks.com
Facebook: Miss Anna Lumpy
Instagram: Miss Anna

Paperback: ISBN 978-1-945977-01-5

Printed in the U.S.A. 1 3 5 7 9 10 8 6 4 2

Author Bio

Miss Anna (Jieeun Jeanne Woo)

Let us write.
Let us draw.
Let us create for all.
Learning should be fun.
The half-steps have begun.
Oh, to see them smile, lil' ones big and small.

- Miss Anna

MISS ANNA writes for her four boys. They are her inspiration to present knowledge in new, creative ways—ways that will help knowledge stay. She writes from her home in the beautiful and green Portland, Oregon.

THE NUMBER STORY

BOOK FOUR

Numbers Teach Children Their Ordinal Names

written and illustrated by

MISS ANNA

For my parents who have cradled me
and have held my hand,

My parents to whom I owe my very being
and memories that have woven into me,

To them I dedicate this book
with my deepest love and gratitude.

Hello!

You have caught us just in time.

We are going on a trip

on this super, flying ship.

We are thrilled,
pleased, and
delighted to go.
You see…

We are going to travel
to see ten grand events.

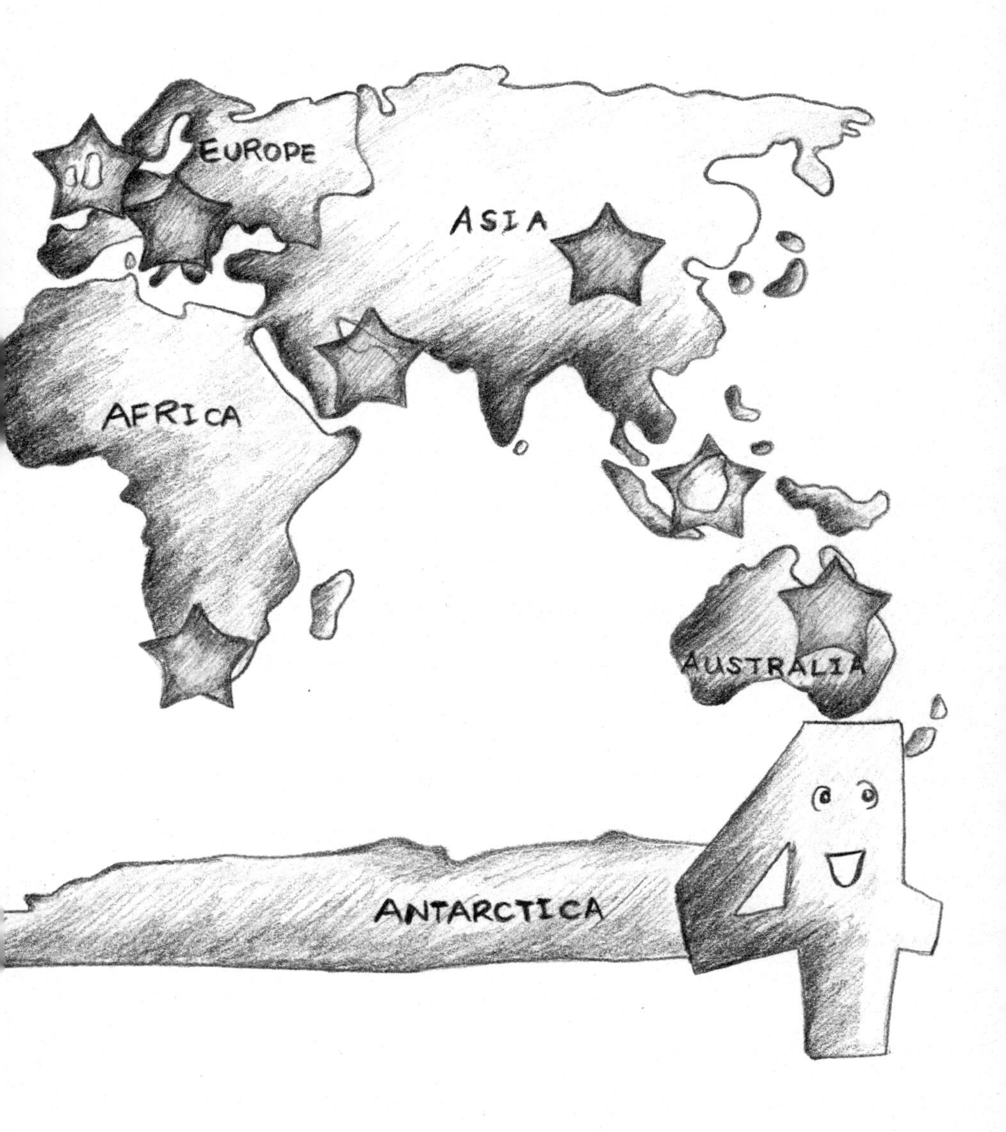

We will visit ten exciting lands
across the seven continents!

Cordially we have been invited,

to contests in yaks and camel racing too.

They need us, so they say,

to decide who won over who.

Yes,
we Numbers
can be helpful,

when counting and
adding up's a problem.

But there's another
job we can do.

We can **organize**
from **top**
to **bottom!**

We can put in order…

The order of floors
in elevators.

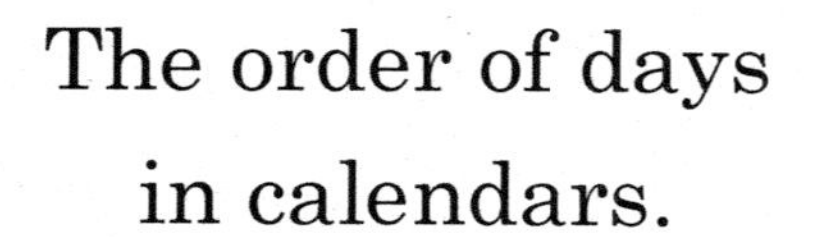

The order of days
in calendars.

The order of rank
and recognition.

The order of place,
sequence, and position.

One, Two, Three —
You already know.

But there's a different name,
a second name.
Turn this page to know.

Now listen very carefully.
HERE WE GO!

Cardinals		*Ordinals*
One		First
Two		Second
Three		Third
Four		Fourth
Five		Fifth

Fun right?

The number ‘three’ is a ‘cardinal’ name.

‘Third’ is an ‘ordinal’ name.

Cardinals		*Ordinals*
Six		Sixth
Seven		Seventh
Eight		Eighth
Nine		Ninth
Ten		Tenth

I know we may seem different,
but we look just the same!

So, let's go on a journey.
Fingers crossed, you'll come along.
It's going to be exciting
to be amongst the cheering throng.

FOR US NUMBERS, OUR JOB IS TO PUT THINGS IN ORDER...
AND TO OUR JOB, STAY TRUE.
ANY CONCERNS OR COMMENTS CALL FOR A CONVERSATION!
WE NUMBERS ARE NOT ENDORSING, ENCOURAGING, or ELEVATING ANY OF THESE GAMES.
CAUTION
CONTROVERSIAL GAMES BEYOND THIS PAGE!

Day 1   1st (First) Day of the Ten-Day Trip

Date: July 11th

Location: North Yorkshire, England

Competition: Knaresborough Bed Race

Up the hills, down the streets,
over the bridge they go.
Carrying their beds, they cross a river,
braving the water flow.

The best dressed team and the fastest team
wins top marks and gets first place.
They run for charity; it is a lot of fun.
There's a smile on every face.

Which team is coming in first – 1st?

Day 2 2nd (Second) Day of the Ten-Day Trip

Date: July 12th

Location: Makarov, Czech Republic

Competition: Downhill Skateboarding/Longboarding

WOOOOSH~

Freeriding is a downhill thrill,
Where a skateboarder tests her speed and skill.

On endless hills of twists and turns,
They jump and skip and tire burns.

Skateboarders drift, curve and slide.
They do it for glory, for the FUN OF THE RIDE!

Which skateboarder is coming in second – 2nd?

Day 3 3rd (Third) Day of the Ten-Day Trip

Date: July 13th

Location: A'Sharqiyah Sands, Oman

Competition: Camel Racing

The one-hump dromedaries are not slow. It's true.
They can run as well as they can spit and chew.

A Bactrian camel visiting from Central Asia.

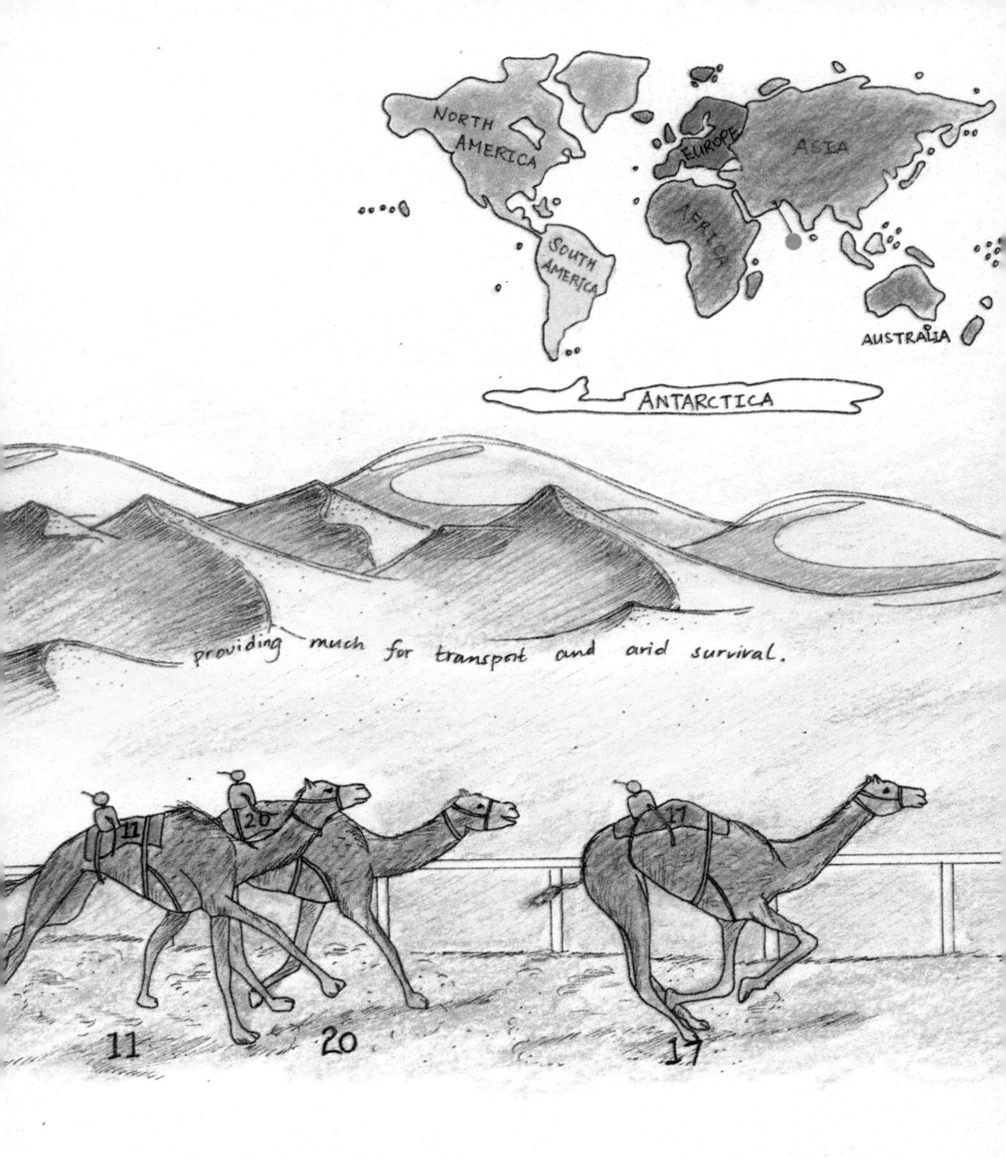

Carrying a robot jockey on a humpy back,
With dust swirling on the sandy track,
The camels sprint shooting for the goal,
Urged on by the owner's robotic remote control.

Which camel is coming in third – 3rd?

Day 4 4th (Fourth) Day of the Ten-Day Trip

Date: July 14th

Location: Oudtshoorn in the Karoo, South Africa

Competition: Ostrich Derby

Standing up to nine feet tall,
With legs so powerful and talons that maul,

An ostrich can run. An ostrich can kill.
So, best not to anger him or provoke his ill will.
The very best jockeys will be riding today.
The birds seem to know them and will *probably* obey.

Wild and untamed, with dogged willpower,
They'll throw up dust as they run at
forty-three miles per hour!

Which ostrich is coming in fourth – 4th?

Day 5 5th (Fifth) Day of the Ten-Day Trip

Date: July 15th

Location: Orkhon Valley in Bat Ulzii Sum, Mongolia

Competition: Yak Racing

We have landed on a nomadic land.
The grassy steppes are wide and grand.

The much-loved yak
is greatly appreciated.

Much help do they give, well, the ones they domesticated.
So during the Yak Festival, which is held every year,
Yak races take place, and the crowds, how they cheer.

Which yak is coming in fifth – 5th?

Day 6 6th (Sixth) Day of the Ten-Day Trip

Date: July 16th

Location: Townsville, Queensland in Australia

Competition: Spartan Race (Obstacle Race)

The Spartan Race is an obstacle course,
with mud, monkey bars, and barbed wire, of course.
They run, they jump, determined to win.

They scale cargo nets and refuse to give in.
This race is for the bold.
This race is for the strong,
who shows spirit and strength, to go on and on.

Which Spartan
is coming in sixth – 6th?

Day 7 7th (Seventh) Day of the Ten-Day Trip

Date: July 17th
Location: Jakarta, Indonesia
Competition: Panjat Pinang (Climbing Nut Tree) Competition

Slippery, greasy, messy, and muddy,

With everyday gifts
to titillating luxury,

The poles stand erect, but the contestants stand tall.
They all work together, refusing to fall.

Which team do you think is in seventh – 7th place?
Hmmm... This is a tricky race.

Day 8 8th (Eighth) Day of the Ten-Day Trip

Date: July 18th

Location: Easter Island west of Chile

Competition: Haka Pei in the Rapa Nui Tapati Festival

For two days, the Rapa Nuis sing and dance,
to the powerful drumming of the tribal chants.

Among the highlights is Haka Pei.
Men slide down on a banana-trunk sleigh.
You mean THAT steep hill which is long as a mile?
YUP! It is a hair-raising sport in Easter Isle.

Which banana-trunk sleigh do you think will be coming in eighth—8th?

Who do you think will go the farthest? Hmmm… They are all going so fast!

Day 9 **9th (Ninth) Day** of the Ten-Day-Trip

Date: July 19th

Location: Wiamic, Oregon in North America

Competition: Lawn Mower Racing

What is THAT going around?

Do you hear that vrrroooming sound?

Lawn mowers designed to trim, cut and slice,

Now transformed into sports cars spruced up with spice...

With the blade torn away, the engine souped-up,

Mowers cross fingers that they'll win the cup.

'But it's not about winning,' many mowers declare.
'It is more about TINKERING
and the adventure we share.'

Which lawnmower is coming in ninth – 9th?

Day 10 **10th (Tenth) Day** of the Ten-Day Trip

Date: July 20th

Location: Sisimiut, Greenland

Competition: The Arctic Cross Country Skiing

A three-day race across snow and ice.
100 miles of rugged paradise.
Camping, sleeping, and cooking on the way,
Racers stay on the path lest they wander and stray.

It is a tough cross country, the toughest of all!
Who knows what might happen,
who knows who will fall.

Skiing and competing over
mountainous terrains

Aluu!

Can cause spasm
and sprains
and light-headed
brains.

But the joy for the sport
brings people here.
And, with the finish in sight, they cry and they cheer.

Which racer is coming in tenth – 10th?

Oh, the games were so much fun.
Well done! Well done!
To EVERYONE.

Putting things in order was a *whiz*.
And the Ordinals were honored
to be of service.

With our job done,
we can finally look around.

Whoa! Is Eight excited.

“This airship is
a ten-story
PLAYGROUND!”

Finally!
Let’s take a tour.
There must a
a restaurant

somewhere for sure.

WELCOME
to The Ordinals!
THE GLASS SKY ROOM
REST ROOM
9th
ninth
KITCHEN
THE GREEN IN THE BLUE
SHOWER ROOM
7th
seventh
MINI GOLF
JUMP IN THE CLOUDS
5th
fifth
CAPTAIN AND THE CREWS' QUARTERS
ART STUDIO
3rd
third
ICE CREAM IN THE SKY
Wow! ice cream
1st
first
CONTROL ROOM

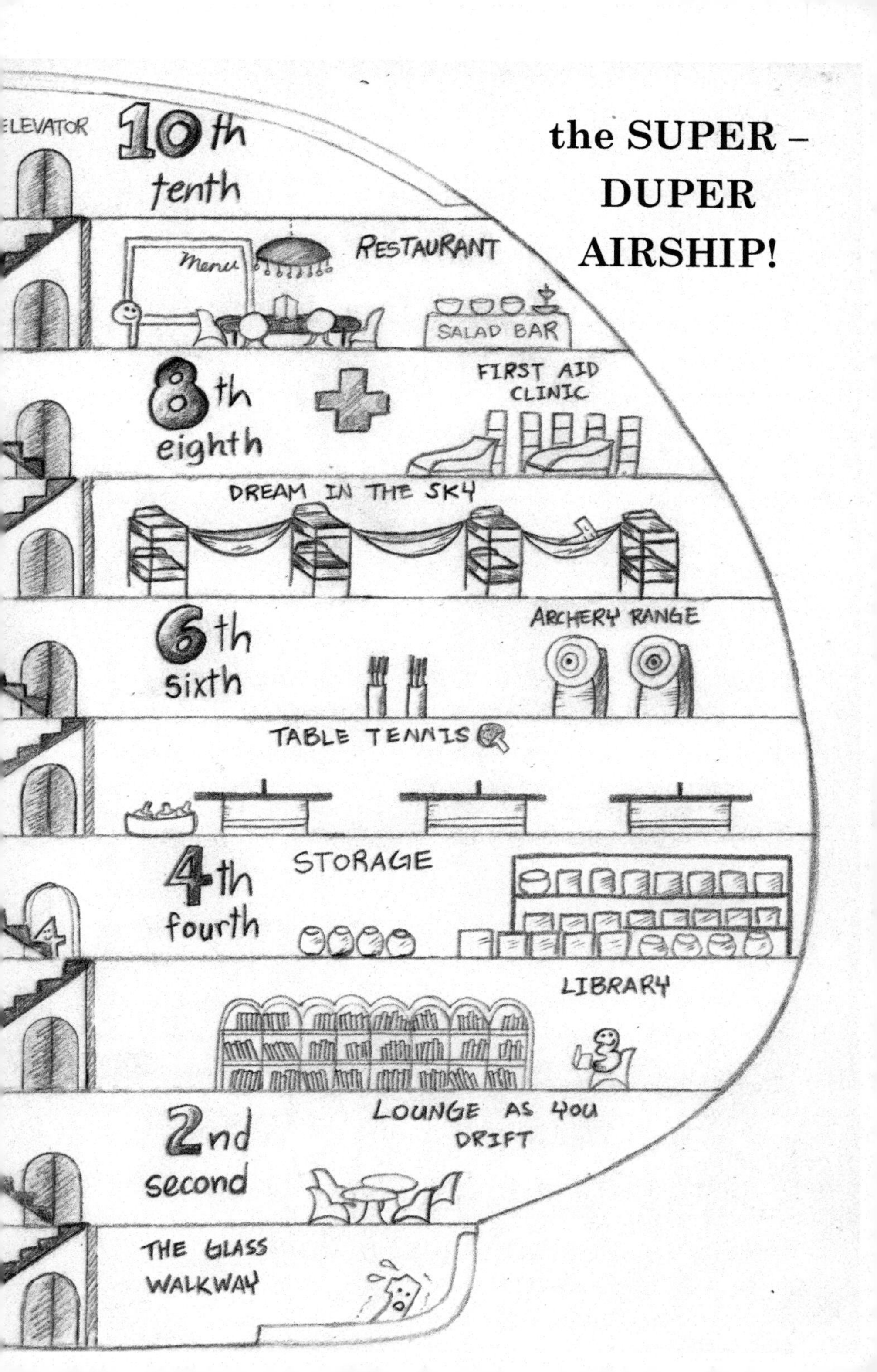

ELEVATOR
10th
tenth
RESTAURANT
Menu
SALAD BAR
8th
eighth
FIRST AID
CLINIC
DREAM IN THE SKY
6th
sixth
ARCHERY RANGE
TABLE TENNIS
4th
fourth
STORAGE
LIBRARY
2nd
second
LOUNGE AS YOU
DRIFT
THE GLASS
WALKWAY
the SUPER –
DUPER
AIRSHIP!

Alas,

We Numbers must say adieu for now.

So, we wave, we grin,

we take one final bow.

But do remember,

When you need a super ‘sorter’,

To put things like sports cars

in numerical order,

Think of us.
We are here.
We Ordinals are faithful
every day and every year.

Our names may be different,

THE
SAME!

I'M the FIRST!
NO, YOU'RE NOT.
FIRST
YOU ARE the ZEROST! KK